YOUNG-LUV.COM

STAYC

STAYC The 2nd Mini Album

YOUNG-LUV.COM

STAYC

YOUNG-LUV.COM

STAYC

RUN2U

RUN! / Told you not 또 괜한 기대 겉으론 걱정해 난 안 바뀌네 또 가끔 말을 막 해 너무 딱해 헛소리들 나는 안 들리네 no oh yeah Told you 난 so always b day 겉으론 내 편인데 못해 이해 그 참견들은 가짜 나는 바빠 어떻게 해도 나는 안 들리네 no no oh / 타 버리고 파 너의 사랑은 so sunny yeah 사라져도 사라져도 다 버리고 파 너만 있다면 no worry yeah 알잖아 It should be you / So I'LL RUN TO YOU So I'LL RUN TO YOU 선을 넘는 거래도 over and over 다쳐도 괜찮아 I'LL RUN TO YOU / So I'LL RUN TO YOU A little bit little bit (Young) A little bit little bit (Young) A little bit little bit 알지 나의 Style / 네가 어떤 너래도 over and over 다쳐도 괜찮아 I'LL RUN TO YOU / JJ 물불 안 가리는 type I never 절대로 도도 망가질 수 없는 사이 알잖아 I'm not a poser / 혹시라도 잘못돼도 절대 너를 탓하지 않아 그게 어디라도 wanna be there / 타 버리고 파 너의 사랑은 so sunny yeah 사라져도 사라져도 다 버리고 파 너만 있다면 no worry yeah 알잖아 It should be you / So I'LL RUN TO YOU So I'LL RUN TO YOU 선을 넘는 거래도 over and over 다쳐도 괜찮아 I'LL RUN TO YOU / So I'LL RUN TO YOU / A little bit little bit (Young) A little bit little bit (Young) A little bit little bit 알지 나의 Style / 네가 어떤 너래도 over and over 다쳐도 괜찮아 I'LL RUN TO YOU / No no that's ok that's ok 누가 뭐래도 No 괜찮아 아플 거래도 / 상관없어 멋대로 생각해도 돼 막지 못해 널 사랑하기 때문에 / So I'LL RUN TO YOU So I'LL RUN TO YOU 선을 넘는 거래도 over and over 다쳐도 괜찮아 I'LL RUN TO YOU / So I'LL RUN TO YOU / A little bit little bit (Young) A little bit little bit (Young) A little bit little bit / 알지 나의 Style / 네가 어떤 너래도 over and over 다쳐도 괜찮아 I'LL RUN TO YOU

STAYC

YOUNG-LUV.COM

Composed by B.E.P, Jeon goon, FLYT
Lyrics by B.E.P, Jeon goon
Arranged by Rado, FLYT

Drums by Rado
Keyboard by FLYT
Bass by FLYT
Chorus by 시은 (STAYC), Rado
Recorded by 정은경 @ingrid studio
Digital editing by 정은경 @ingrid studio
Mixed by DRK (Assist 김준상, 지민우)
@koko sound studio
Mastered by Stuart Hawkes @Metropolis Mastering Studios

SAME SAME 우리 둘의 마음은 같아
달라질 건 없을 것 같아 애써 시간만 끌어
봤자 Baby I don't wanna waste
my time / 그래 우린 SAME SAME
/ I know I know 빨리 말해줘 감추려고
해도 티가 나는 걸 아닌 척하느라 바쁘네
헛수고야 cause I know already
/ 갑자기 손을 잡아도 좋아 눈빛으로
대신해도 좋아 그게 꼭 말이 아니면 어때
Baby boy you better hurry up
/ SAME SAME 우리 둘의 마음은
같아 달라질 건 없을 것 같아 애써 시간만
끌어 봤자 Baby I don't wanna
waste my time / 그래 우린 SAME
SAME / 참 못 말려 나도 참 못돼 No
never 내가 먼저 말 못 해 Please
오해하지 말고 들어 get it right 솔직히
나 답답해서 죽겠어 / 갑자기 날 안아줘도
좋아 분위기로 대신해도 좋아 그게 꼭 말이
아니면 어때 Baby boy you better
hurry up / SAME SAME 우리
둘의 마음은 같아 달라질 건 없을 것 같아
애써 시간만 끌어 봤자 Baby I don't
wanna waste my time / 쉽지 않은
거 나도 아는데 (Listen my boy) 먼저
다가와 줘 네가 먼저 말해줘 / Same
oh same oh same 똑같은 맘인데
No way no way no 먼저 말 못 해
오래오래 못 기다려줘 Better hurry
up oh 우린 이미 똑같아 / Same
oh same oh same 똑같은 맘인데
No way no way no 먼저 말 못 해
오래오래 못 기다려줘 / STAYC girls
it's going down

YOUNG-LUV.COM

Composed by B.E.P, Jeon goon
Lyrics by B.E.P, Jeon goon
Arranged by Rado

Drums by Rado
Bass by Rado
Keyboard by Rado
Chorus by 시은 (STAYC)
Recorded by 정은경 @ingrid studio
Digital editing by 정은경 @ingrid studio
Mixed by DRK (Assist 김준상, 지민우)
@koko sound studio
Mastered by Stuart Hawkes @Metropolis
Mastering Studios

TRACK 2
SAME SAME

TRACK 3
247

STAYC

Composed by BXN
Lyrics by BXN
Arranged by BXN

Drums by 좌행석
Keyboard by 이길범
Chorus by 시은 (STAYC)
Recorded by 정은경
@ingrid studio
Digital editing by 정은경
@ingrid studio
Mixed by DRK
(Assist 김준상, 지민우)
@koko sound studio
Mastered by Stuart Hawkes
@Metropolis Mastering
Studios

You got me you got me you got me / I'll never take you nowhere nowhere 널 내 곁에만 둘래 몰래 너와 이렇게 24/7 with you 그대로 24/7 with you / Got me goin' goin' 너만의 baby Oh 길들여졌어 Can't nobody be like you I know that can't nobody be like you / 시간이 흐른대도 어디에 있다 해도 계속 네 곁에 with you / 손을 놓지 않을게 너도 같은 마음인 듯해 My baby You shouldn't go / Baby tell me what you want Whatever you want 모두 이뤄줄게 baby 네가 원하는 것 갖고 싶은 것 Oh 내게만 말해줄래 / 널 위해 준비한 선물 너 아닌 그 누구도 모를 네가 원하는 것 갖고 싶은 것 My 24/7 24/7 you / You're so, You're so Different different 24/7 with you 24/7 with you / 시간은 넘쳐나 기분은 뭐랄까 어디로든 떠날까 밤이 오고 해가 뜰 때까지 계속 달려도 괜찮아 / 도망가자 지금 아주 먼 데로 저 멀리 Montero 우리를 알아보는 사람 없는 곳으로 / You got me you got me you got me / 시간이 멈춘대도 모두가 다 변해도 계속 네 곁에 with you / 손을 놓지 않을게 너도 같은 마음인 듯해 My baby You shouldn't go / Trippin', look what you started it Keep on, nothing cannot stop me 하루 종일 보고 있어도 전혀 안 지겨워 Want it all want it all 아이처럼 Dream on you, trip on you 맘에 반쪽 아닌 전부를 다 줘 색안경은 벗고 날 봐줘 deep inside me / Baby tell me what you want Whatever you want 모두 이뤄줄게 baby 네가 원하는 것 갖고 싶은 것 Oh 내게만 말해줄래 / 널 위해 준비한 선물 너 아닌 그 누구도 모를 네가 원하는 것 갖고 싶은 것 My 24/7 24/7 you / Baby Baby 널 내 곁에만 둘래 몰래 너와 이렇게 24/7 with you 그대로 24/7 with you / Got me goin' goin' 너만의 baby baby 이렇게 24/7 with you 영원히 24/7 with you

My love's so young I'm young 달콤한 나이 너만 바라볼 순 없어 na na na na Cold I'm cold 깜깜한 밤 아름답긴 해도 따뜻하진 않아 / Ooh ooh ooh ooh 겉으로만 나 멀쩡한 거 일지도 Ooh ooh ooh ooh 쟀든 baby I'm sorry for my YOUNG LUV / 몰라도 돼 복잡한 나의 태도 떠나도 돼 It doesn't really matter 혼자 몰래 눈물 흘리게 돼도 절대로 변하지 않아 you'll never know / 상처만 남고서 무너져 fallin 떠올리고 싶지 않아 no no no 나빠도 괜찮아 do it just for me 잘 들어줘 you gotta know that / My love's so young I'm young 달콤한 나이 너만 바라볼 순 없어 na na na na Cold I'm cold 깜깜한 밤 아름답긴 해도 따뜻하진 않아 / Ooh ooh ooh ooh 겉으로만 나 멀쩡한 거 일지도 Ooh ooh ooh ooh 쟀든 baby I'm sorry for my YOUNG LUV / 말론 늘 모든 걸 전부 줄 것처럼 해 흔들리지 않아 I'm strong / 어설프게 다가와서 사랑인 척해 다시 나는 속지 않아 you know I'm so bad / 혼자만 남겨져 눈물이 fallin 기억하고 싶지 않아 no no 아프기 싫잖아 do it just for me 잘 들어줘 you gotta know that / My love's so young I'm young 달콤한 나이 너만 바라볼 순 없어 na na na na Cold I'm cold 깜깜한 밤 아름답긴 해도 따뜻하진 않아 / 만약에 만약에 내가 정말 다시 돌아갈 수 있을까 처음 봐 차갑게 차갑게 식은 내 맘 Don't you act like you don't know at all / My love's so young I'm young 달콤한 나이 너만 바라볼 순 없어 na na na na / Cold I'm cold 깜깜한 밤 아름답긴 해도 따뜻하진 않아 / Ooh ooh ooh ooh 겉으로만 나 멀쩡한 거 일지도 Ooh ooh ooh ooh 쟀든 baby I'm sorry for my YOUNG LUV

TRACK 4

YOUNG LUV

STAYC

Drums by FLYT
Keyboard by FLYT
Piano by FLYT
Chorus by STAYC, Rado, Jeon goon, FLYT
Recorded by 정은경 @ingrid studio
Digital editing by 정은경 @ingrid studio
Mixed by DRK (Assist 김준상, 지민우) @koko sound studio
Mastered by Stuart Hawkes @Metropolis Mastering Studios

Composed by B.E.P, Jeon goon, FLYT
Lyrics by B.E.P, Jeon goon
Arranged by FLYT

BUTTERFLY

STAYC

BUTTERFLY 그 어떤 별보다도 빛나는 너를 / BUTTERFLY 날 밝혀주는 작은 빛 little love It's you / 아무런 이유 없어 널 사랑했던 건 빛이 눈부셔서 Ooh yeah / 이유가 되어줬어 너란 존재만으로 저 하늘을 꿈꾸게 했어 / My little love little love stay Cause you know my You know my way 수많은 구름들 사이 널 찾을 수 있게 / Who knew Oh 언제든 어디서든 널 알아볼 수 있게 그 모습 그대로 Fly ooh / BUTTERFLY 그 어떤 별보다도 빛나는 너를 / BUTTERFLY 날 밝혀주는 작은 빛 little love It's you / 일상이 됐어 널 기억하는 것 상상하는 것 하나하나 다 / I'm just thinkin 'bout you I'm crazy 'bout you 밤새 그저 바라볼 / 새까만 우주 속에 불빛 왠지 너를 닮은 작은 Satellite / Oh stay Cause you know my You know my way 짙어진 하늘 그 사이 널 찾을 수 있게 / Who knew Oh 언제든 어디서든 널 찾아낼 수 있게 그 모습 그대로 Shine bright / 흩날리는 조각 잎과 바람들 and you 아름다운 날갯짓으로 / 그저 눈부시게 높이 날아줘 my love 너와 나의 세상 속에서 / BUTTERFLY 저 구름 위의 별처럼 빛난다면 I know baby it's you / BUTTERFLY 날 밝혀주는 작은 빛 little love It's you / BUTTERFLY You're all mine / BUTTERFLY

YOUNG-LUV.COM

Composed by BXN, Prime Time
Lyrics by BXN
Arranged by BXN

Drums by 좌행석
Keyboard by 이길범
Piano by 변무혁
Chorus by 시은 (STAYC)
Recorded by 정은경 @ingrid studio
Digital Edited by 정은경 @ingrid studio
Mixed by DRK (Assist 김준상, 지민우)
@koko sound studio
Mastered by Stuart Hawkes
@Metropolis Mastering Studios

I WANT YOU BABY

STAYC

On my head In my face 홀린 건지 꿈인 건지 oh 이상해 잠에서 뒤척이다 깰 때도 웃음이 나 그날의 말 오늘도 / 언제부터일까 insane 어려웠던 우리 사인 마치 mathematic / Now I feel I'm floating all day 모든 게 떠있는 것 같아 꿈만 같아 yeah / I WANT YOU BABY 별을 헤는 밤 별을 따다 줄 널 원해 Just want you baby 비워진 내 맘 가득 담아 줄 널 원해 I love ya / Cause I'm crazy in love Crazy in love I'm crazy in love Crazy in love with star / I WANT YOU BABY 오늘 같은 밤 I knew that you were thinking 'bout me / Hey my babe Watch me babe Oh 암말 없이 보기만도 좋은 걸 귀찮은 건 없어 너와의 관계는 움직여져 모든 게 다 네게로 / 가까이 와 널 보고 싶어 매일 어디든 날 찾아와 like the mage / And come into my heart 셀 수 없을 만큼 안고 싶어 안고 싶어 yeah / I WANT YOU BABY 별을 헤는 밤 별을 따다 줄 널 원해 Just want you baby 비워진 내 맘 가득 담아 줄 널 원해 I love ya / Cause I'm crazy in love Crazy in love I'm crazy in love Crazy in love with star / I WANT YOU BABY 오늘 같은 밤 I knew that you were thinking 'bout me / 오늘 이 밤 끝나겠지만 I'm fine 너와 나 둘을 비춰줄 거야 사랑은 좀 서툴겠지만 all right / You could be my only star / I WANT YOU BABY 별을 헤는 밤 별이 되어 줄 널 원해 (I love you) / Just want you baby 채워질 내 맘 한껏 안아 줄 널 원해 I love ya / Cause I'm crazy in love Crazy in love I'm crazy in love Crazy in love with star / I WANT YOU BABY 오늘 같은 밤 I knew that you were thinking 'bout me

Composed by will.b
Lyrics by will.b, van.gogh
Arranged by will.b

Bass by will.b
Midi programing by will.b
Chorus by STAYC
Recorded by 정은경, 양영은 @ingrid studio
Digital Edited by 정은경 @ingrid studio
Mixed by DRK (Assist 김준상, 지민우)
@koko sound studio
Mastered by Stuart Hawkes
@Metropolis Mastering Studios

YOUNG-LUV.COM

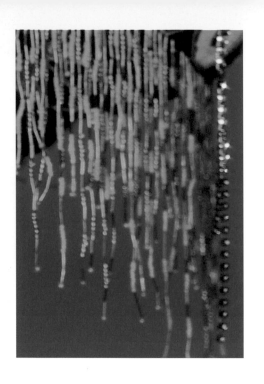

STAYC The 2nd Mini Album
YOUNG-LUV.COM

STAYC The 2nd Mini Album
YOUNG-LUV.COM

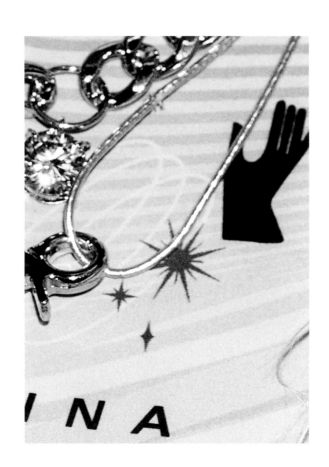

STAYC The 2nd Mini Album
YOUNG-LUV.COM

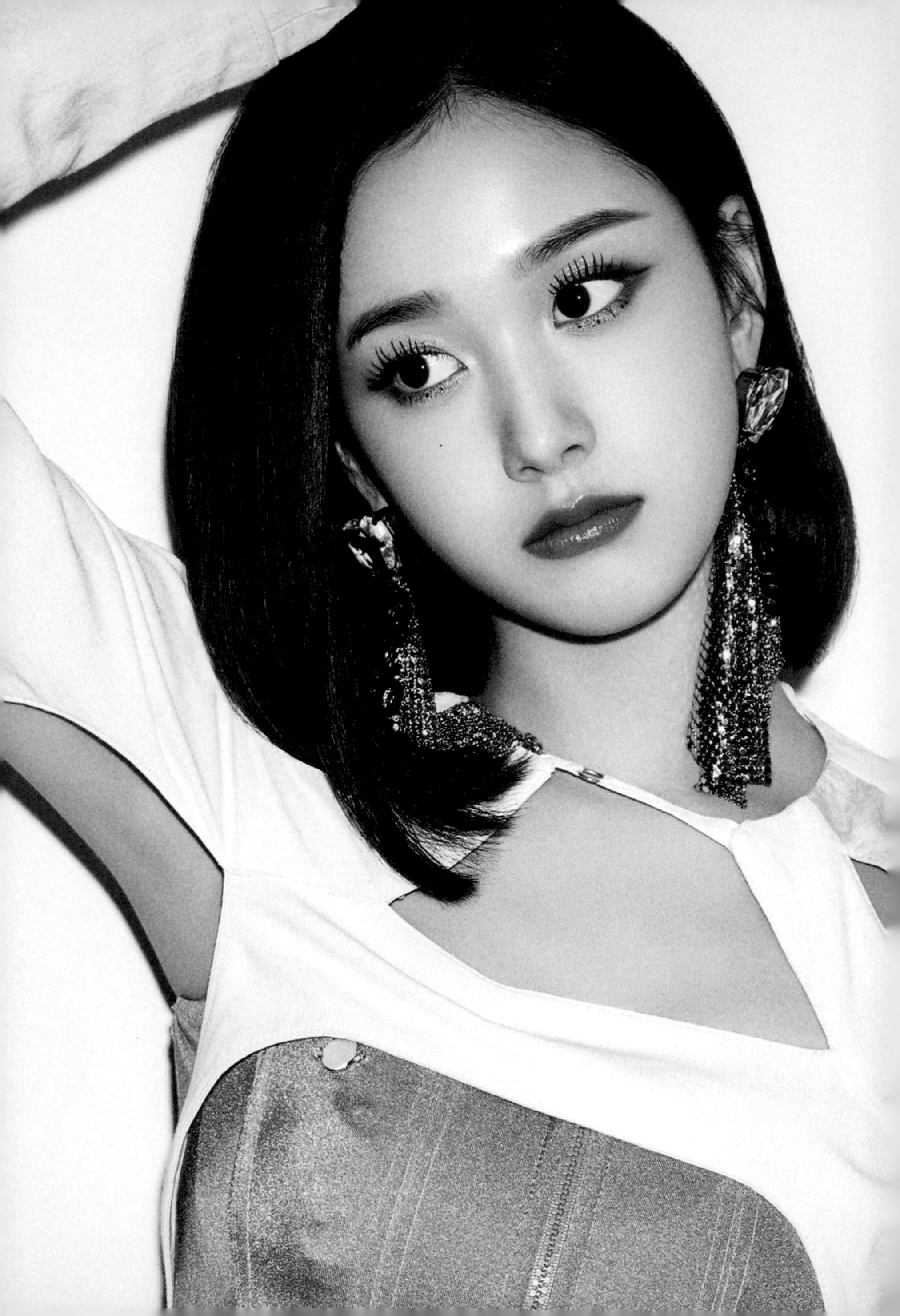

STAYC The 2nd Mini Album
YOUNG-LUV.COM

STAYC The 2nd Mini Album
YOUNG-LUV.COM

High Up Entertainment

Artist STAYC
Executive Producer B.E.P
Co-producer Jeon goon
Executive Supervisor Michael Choi
Executive Director Mr.sangun
Creative Director Rado
Chief Manager Dustin Kim
A&R Jeong Jun Hyeon
Artist Development & Casting Dustin Kim, Lee Jae Eun, Kim Sol
Planning Lee Jae Eun
Production Lee Su Ha, Park Eun Joo
Marketing Jeong Hee Ra, Park Ji Hye
Contents Production Jung Bora, Park Young Shin, Kang Yeong Min, Woo Yu Lim
Finance & Administration Choo Yoon Hee, An Hyeon Seon
Artist Management Kwon Jun Mo, Choi In Hyuck, Seong Yeong Chan, Lee Seong Je
Advertising Business Oh Ji Ho
Global Business Xiao Han
Public Relations HNS HQ

Music Video Director WOOGIE KIM @MOTHER MEDIA
Performance by 이유종, 고경준, 이제민 @CODE88 채다솜 @freemind
Photograph JANG DUKHWA
Art Shin Hoseung 신호승 @summerskythunderstorm
Art Team 우제이슨 @ouu_jason, 김하영 @hayoungkeem
Balloon Art 김태윤 Taeyoon Kim @balloon_sepo
Lighting KIM MINSOO
Album Design by 나래 @studiograey
Cover Artwork by May Kim, Yann Cavaille @May Kim Production
Make-up 오길주, 박혜민, 이선영, 장한별 @ALUU
Hair 이민아, 김도영, 김현지, 이현아, 이인영 @ALUU
Stylist 홍하리
Stylist Assist 김엘림 조수빈 김세린 @team.punksnotdead
Recording Engineer 정은경, 양영은 @ingrid studio
Mixed by DRK (Assist 김준상, 지민우) @koko sound studio
Mastered by Stuart Hawkes @Metropolis Mastering Studios
Printed by Yein-Art

STAYC